Books are to be returned on or before
the last date below.

- - DEC 2007

LIBREX-

POPULATION CHANGE

Elizabeth Tyndall

W

FRANKLIN WATTS

LONDON • SYDNEY

First published in 2007 by Franklin Watts
338 Euston Road, London NW1 3BH

Franklin Watts Australia
Level 17/207 Kent Street
Sydney NSW 2000

Editor: Julia Bird
Designer: Thomas Keenes
Picture researcher: Sarah Smithies

Picture credits:
Cover: PCL/Alamy: 21. Mark
Pearson/Alamy: 22. Philip Bigg/Alamy: 25.
Adam van Bunnens /Alamy: 7. Age
Concern: 27 (t). Ariel Skelley/Corbis: 27 (b).
Chris Ballentine/Paul Thompson
Images/Alamy: 18. Folio Photography: 15.
Gideon Mendel/Corbis: 4. John
Garrett/Corbis: 10. Jonathan Hordle/Rex
Features: 24. Matthew Fearn/PA/Empics: 6.
Michael Freeman/Corbis: 9. Network
Photographers/Alamy: 17. Nicholas
Bailey/Rex Features: 23. Paul Hardy/Corbis:
19. PCL/Alamy: 21. PictureNet/Corbis: 14.
Popperfoto/Alamy: 13. Private
Collection/Bridgeman Art Library: 8.
Rex Features: 29.

A CIP catalogue record for this book
is available from the British Library

ISBN: 978 0 7496 7600 1

Dewey Classification: 304.6'0941

Printed in China

Franklin Watts is a division of
Hachette Children's Books,
an Hachette Livre UK company.

CONTENTS

BRITAIN'S CHANGING FACES

Population change can transform the places that we live in. The composition and density of an area's population shape where people live within Britain, the way in which we earn money, and even our life expectancy.

Controversial change

Population change is not always welcome. Tension can result when one population group becomes larger than another, or when laws are passed which appear to favour one group over another. In recent years, there has been controversy over the number of immigrants arriving in Britain.

| Births | + | Immigrants | – | Deaths | – | Emigrants | = Population |

▲ 'Natural change' is the difference between the number of births and deaths within a given time. This, combined with immigration and emigration, gives us our total population.

In the past, there was tension between Protestant and Catholic groups, after laws that restricted Catholic land inheritance and ownership were lifted.

People, policy and planning

As individuals, population change affects us in matters such as competition for jobs and housing. As a wider social group, population change influences how we use up and allocate resources and has an impact on our performance globally. Policy-makers use information about the demographics of a population – for example the numbers of adults relative to children and the range of ethnic groups in a community – to make important decisions on matters such as health, education and housing.

A 'population policy'?

Some people believe population change is so important that Britain should have a dedicated 'population policy'. Such a policy would influence decisions about the population's composition and number. For example, if we knew we wanted a larger labour force in the future, a 'population policy' might encourage more people to have babies today. Critics of such a policy claim it would lead to too much interference by the government in personal decisions, such as how many children a family decides to have.

◄ The British population is made up of a diverse mix of ethnicities. Immigration has played a huge part in this.

JUST THE FACTS

In Britain from 2004-05:

● the total population was 60,209,500.

● the average age was 38.8 years.

● 717,500 babies were born.

● 590,600 people died.

● approximately 223,000 more people migrated to Britain than migrated abroad.

MEASURING CHANGE

More than 60 million faces, and just one central government. How do we keep up with the unique life stories that contribute to Britain's ever-changing population?

Monitoring the population

Every time someone fills out a form or answers a questionnaire, he or she adds to information that businesses, health authorities, transport and housing services and the government use to analyse common population trends and plan for the future. But only two systems uniformly monitor people's lives. The census and civil registration schemes allow us to examine and cross-reference population tendencies across Britain.

◄ The census is long and time-consuming to complete. It is necessary to balance the importance of the information gathered with people's willingness to participate.

Census

The census is an immense undertaking, completed every ten years by the Office of National Statistics in England and Wales, the General Register Office in Scotland and the Statistics and Research Agency in Northern Ireland. Every household in Britain is required by law to answer questions about its demographics, such as age, sex and ethnicity, and lifestyle matters.

Counting the cost

The 2001 census cost approximately £255 million. Some argue that this massive expense is not justifiable. The amount of information gathered takes time to

JUST THE FACTS

- The first census was conducted in 1801.

- 70,000 field workers helped capture information in the 2001 census, delivering census forms to every household and establishment in Britain.

- The 2001 census contained 41 questions (42 in Wales where a question about the Welsh language was included).

- 94% of households completed a census form in 2001.

assemble and examine, and by the time it is used to assist in policy decisions, it may be out of date. Besides, much of the information is already held in different forms elsewhere. But no other system allows data to be compared across local, regional and national levels.

Civil registration

A more immediate measure of population change is the civil register. Every birth, death and marriage is recorded as it happens. This register is also used to confirm personal identity for proof of nationality, age or marital status.

Up for discussion

In the future, it will be the law that all British residents carry an identity card. These would be linked to a database holding information about every person in the country. What do you think could be some of the benefits and problems associated with this?

▼ This couple is signing the marriage register. Changes in marriage rates can help to predict other trends, such as birth rates.

PEOPLE IN THE PAST

In 1750, Britain had a population of six million. By 1920, less than 200 years later, the population had soared to 42 million.

Industrial revolution

At the heart of this population explosion was the Industrial Revolution, which began in around 1760. This shift from an economy based around manual labour and simple craftsmanship to an economy based around power-driven machinery and industry transformed Britain. People began enjoying prosperity like never before. Higher living standards and better access to basic resources, such as food and medical treatment, caused both an increase in births and a drop in death rates.

▼ **Population Explosion, 1700 – 1931**
Official population counts only started with the first census in 1801. Estimates of population totals before that were based on records of baptisms, burials and marriages.

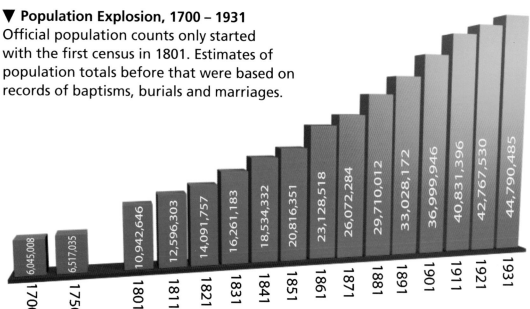

Year	Population
1700	6,045,008
1750	6,517,035
1801	10,942,646
1811	12,596,303
1821	14,091,757
1831	16,261,183
1841	18,534,332
1851	20,816,351
1861	23,128,518
1871	26,072,284
1881	29,710,012
1891	33,028,172
1901	36,999,946
1911	40,831,396
1921	42,767,530
1931	44,790,485

CASE STUDY
The Doomsday Book

Historians continually search for evidence about life and populations past. The Doomsday Book gives a fascinating insight into life in Britain in the 11th century. It was commissioned in 1086 by the Norman king William the Conqueror to find out how much land was owned in England, and by whom, so he knew how much tax he could charge. It was the first ever attempt at collecting information about the population on this scale and gives us extensive detail about people's lives at the time.

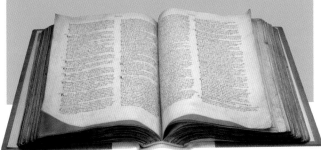

◄ Many people in the early 19th century lived in slum conditions like these, which helped diseases to spread fast.

The urban squeeze

One result of the economic boom was a rapid shift from rural to urban living, as people hurried to the cities to fill new jobs. Between 1800 and 1850 the British urban population doubled and this created a host of new problems. Suddenly thousands of people were forced to live in cramped rooms overlooking dirty streets. Diseases such as cholera, tuberculosis and typhus spread quickly, caused by people living in close proximity without adequate sanitation. Death rates were especially high for children and infants.

Living conditions reform

The British government watched in alarm as death rates rose, starting to link them with recent changes in living conditions. Throughout the 1830s and 40s, sanitary reformers advised the government on basics such as providing fresh water, and disposing of sewage. Adequate housing for the workers fuelling the economic revolution also became a new priority for the government. Slowly, diseases came under control and death rates dropped, with the result that the population grew ever more rapidly.

POPULATION AT WORK

A country relies on its workers to build wealth, and people need to work to support themselves and their families. But it can prove to be a delicate balancing act.

Finding the balance

Growing populations, with many people of working age, stimulate and support industry. People living in successful economies have a longer life expectancy, and birth rates tend to be high. However, too large a population can mean:
● lots of competition for resources, such as food and housing
● more complicated and expensive infrastructures for basic services such as transport and electricity
● overcrowding, which can lead to unrest.

JUST THE FACTS

● About 1 in 5 jobs in Britain are now in the finance and business services, compared with about 1 in 10 in 1981.

● In 1981, men filled 3.2 million more jobs than women. Now it is almost equal, with men performing 12.8 million jobs and women 12.7 million (although almost half of these are part time).

● In 1978, there were 7,124,000 jobs in manufacturing in Britain. In 2005 this had more than halved to only 3,383,000.

Too few people, in the case of a diminishing population, or even a stable population, can mean:
● fewer workers to contribute to industry
● a downfall in a country's economic impact worldwide
● a higher number of elderly dependents relative to the workers who must support them.

These effects can sometimes be seen within individual cities, as well as nationwide.

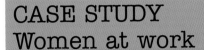

CASE STUDY
Women at work

Prior to the 1970s, few women in Britain worked once they had married and started a family. However, following a global economic slump in the 1970s, the British government actively encouraged women to work. They offered maternity allowances and encouraged flexible working to help women balance work with caring for their family. This helped start to change the population's attitudes to working women.

Working in modern Britain

Until recently, Britain was best known for its manufacturing and mining industries which were found mostly in the north and west. Since the 1980s, there has been a shift to service industries, such as banking and finance, which are based mainly in the south. People without jobs in the north migrated south to find work. This has left many northern towns suffering the effects of a declining population.

Work to live

Attitudes towards work are also changing. In the past, people tended to work for one organisation for their whole career, whereas now it is common to try many kinds of jobs. More people are also more focused on life outside work, trying to limit working hours to spend more time with family or to pursue other interests.

◀ People protest at the closure of a coal mine in Durham. The disappearance of coal mines across Britain in the 1970s and 80s marked Britain's transition to a service-based economy.

CHANGING FAMILIES

How many people are there in your family? How about your friends? Your teachers? It is likely that for each of you the idea of 'family' means something different.

The new family

In recent decades, Britain has seen a range of different family types and sizes become more common and socially accepted. Our new households include civil partnerships, single-parent families, those regrouped after divorce or separation, families without children, and people living alone.

Why did we change?

In the late 1970s, for the first time since records began, there was a drop in population through natural change. In 1965 the birth rate averaged around 850,000 per year; by 1985 it had dropped to 630,000. Britain was in financial recession and the bleak outlook caused many to delay marriage and starting a family. Between 1972 and 1982 the marriage rate dropped by 20 per cent.

At the same time, a changing moral climate also prompted an increase in people living together outside marriage. More children were born out of wedlock, resulting in more single parent families.

Career women and double incomes

Family size also shrank during the late 1970s. The flagging economy cried out for more workers, and women responded by flowing into the workforce. They started having fewer children later in life, after establishing a career. Parents became accustomed to two incomes, making it difficult to take time out to have children. And the expensive trend for buying houses, rather than renting, caused families to reconsider the cost of children. Many decided not to have children at all.

CASE STUDY
New laws, new attitudes

Laws introduced during the 1960s and 70s made new family forms easier:

● The Family Planning Service was introduced in 1970. This offered advice on contraception and meant more people planned how many children they wanted and when.

● The Divorce Reform Act of 1969 made divorce easier. It allowed couples to divorce on a single ground, such as adultery or unreasonable behaviour. In consequence, the divorce rate doubled from 55,556 in 1969 to 124,556 in 1972.

● The Abortion Act of 1967 legalised abortion under certain conditions up to the 24th week of pregnancy.

► The traditional 'nuclear' family of the 1950s, where the father worked and the mother was expected to stay at home to look after the children.

NEW LIFESTYLES

The way we work and live in Britain has been revolutionised by changes in family structure. The overwhelming trend has been for families to become smaller, causing demand for new kinds of housing. A growing number are now headed by single, working mothers.

Working mothers

The rise of single-parent families has been one of the most important aspects of population change. Some 95 per cent of single-parent families are headed by women, who need to support their

▼ 69 per cent of British women choose to return to work after having children.

Up for discussion

Single mothers can find it hard to secure good childcare while they are at work. How might the government help them?

children. So while greater numbers of female workers contributed to the trend for smaller families, this new trend of women as the sole or chief family breadwinner in turn continued the push for more women to work.

Changing roles

New government policies, regarding maternity pay, childcare support and flexible working hours, have been introduced to help women juggle caring for their families with a career. The government is now reviewing men's roles in helping to care for their families. While paternity conditions are considerably different to those offered to mothers, many flexible working laws, established to help care for families, are available for all.

Lifestyles

As more couples delay starting a family, working instead until their careers are established, they become used to higher disposable incomes. This raises lifestyle expectations and many mothers return to work in order to maintain this standard of living. In turn, this means that children spend a lot of time being cared for by people other than their parents. This social trend has sparked great debate about the quality of childcare available in Britain and the importance of the time a child spends with his or her parents.

Housing

Smaller families mean more households. It is estimated that the total number of households in Britain will increase by 23 per cent from 19.2 million in 1991 to 23.6 million by 2016. This means more housing is needed and the type of housing needed is smaller. The government estimates that in England alone 140,000 new homes need to be built each year to meet demand. Many run-down inner city areas are already being transformed by new housing developments to help meet this need.

CASE STUDY
The Thames Gateway

South-east London is one area being regenerated to provide new homes. The Thames Gateway Project will convert old industrial sites and regenerate existing housing to develop suitable accommodation for all kinds of families. Once complete, it hopes to offer not only housing but also jobs, education, healthcare and entertainment.

▶ The Thames Gateway Project should provide 120,000 new homes by 2012.

LIFE MOVES

One in ten people moved house within Britain in the year before the 2001 census. Work is usually the main reason for people moving around the country.

What is regional migration?

When people relocate from one place in a country to another, it is known as regional migration. Communities are shaped by the arrival of new people and the departure of others. Migration has driven population change in recent years in Britain, as there has been little natural change.

North to south

People live where there is an opportunity to earn a living. Britain's recent major economic shift from manufacturing and mining-based industries, mostly located in the north, to service industries found largely in the south, caused an estimated 374,000 people to move from the north to the south in search of work between 1981 and 2001. However, since the census report in 2001, slightly more people have migrated from southern regions to the rest of Britain, thereby partly reversing this trend.

Young movers

Young adults form the most mobile social group, as they move across the country to attend university or look for employment. Members of this group often have few commitments, such as home-ownership or a family, to tie them to a location.

◄ **Population Density in Britain**
This map shows the variety of population density across Britain. The darker the area, the denser the population. The wealthy south east region of England (including London) contains roughly one third of the British population.

Up for discussion

How do you think the departure of young adults of working age from northern towns and villages might have affected the areas they left behind?

▲ Pensioners enjoying
the sun in Eastbourne, Sussex.

Retirees

The other key social group to move are those shifting from employment to retirement. Retirees are often relatively affluent, having paid off a property, or accumulated savings during their working lives. They look for pleasant surroundings in which to retire, with services tailored to their needs. The current trend in Britain is for this group to head to the south coast, where the climate is relatively mild.

Changes to population structure

Regional migration does not simply change the number of people in a place. It also changes the composition, or structure, of communities. The age of an area's population, its birth rates and its death rates are all affected by who arrives and who leaves. For example, people moving to find jobs are usually of child-bearing age, so as well as securing work in a new place they may also start a family there, increasing the birth rate of the area. By contrast, retired people contribute to the economies of communities by spending their savings in them, but they also increase death rates. An older population also means higher demand for medical care and other support services.

TRADING PLACES

More than 70 per cent of moves within Britain are of a distance of 10km or less. Although small, these population shifts can form trends that change the way we live.

Suburbanisation

In many prosperous countries, there has been a drift from city centres to larger housing developments on the outskirts. This is sometimes known as urban sprawl.

Why suburbia?

Housing in city centres can be cramped and expensive. Many people prefer suburban surroundings to built-up city areas and their associated problems, such as crime, pollution and overcrowding.

A life change is a common reason for people to make their move into suburban areas. When people start a family, they commonly look for bigger properties, near schools and other facilities for children. Retirement is another life stage that might trigger a move to suburban areas, away from former places of employment.

CASE STUDY
Greenbelt policy

Sprawling suburban development alarmed some groups who feared that British countryside and farmland would be engulfed. Britain's 'Greenbelt policy' was introduced in 1955 to restrict housing development in designated 'green' areas. The policy also aimed to help urban regeneration, by encouraging re-development of derelict and other urban land, known as brownfield sites.

Up for discussion

- Some new shopping centres have been built on the outskirts of cities to serve the suburbs. What might be some of the effects of this on inner cities?

- The trend for commuting has created 'sleeper villages'. What do you think these might be?

- Is it more important to protect green areas than to build new houses where people want to live?

Moving to the country

A recent trend in Britain is for people to move to country towns in preference to cities, skipping a move to the suburbs. This is known as counter-urbanisation.

Why choose the country life?

The desirability of suburban areas pushes house prices up. This forces some groups, such as young families, to consider other areas. Many look further afield to country villages. Although they live in the country, many of these groups still work in city centres and travel long distances between work and home each day.

◀ Inner city areas have experienced significant drops in population in previous decades.

▶ Commuters pack London's Liverpool Street Station at rush hour.

City living

However, there is currently a social trend to return to city living. This move has been encouraged by the British government, which offers tax relief for property development in disadvantaged communities and for cleaning up polluted land in urban areas. It has also established Urban Regeneration Companies (URCs), responsible for organising major regeneration projects in urban locations across Britain. If successful, these policies will help to reinvigorate the city centres.

IMMIGRANTS AND EMIGRANTS

Currently, one in 14 Britons is from an ethnic minority. As birth rates in Britain are declining, it is predicted that immigration will be the main source of population growth in the future. Recent changes to European Union (EU) border controls have meant large numbers of immigrants are now arriving in Britain from Europe to find work.

Where do they come from?

Much of Britain's current diversity is a result of policies of the 1950s. To help support the workforce, the government encouraged workers to come to Britain from new Commonwealth countries, such as the West Indies and India. These immigrants often took low-skilled jobs that Britons did not want. Some large organisations, such as the National Health Service (NHS), actively recruited from these countries. Immigration controls have since changed, reducing the numbers arriving from these countries; however the original immigrants have settled in Britain and started families.

Political immigrants

In recent years, asylum seekers and political refugees have become one of the largest groups of immigrants to Britain. Significant groups have included Sri Lankan Tamils, Serbians and Somalis in the 1990s, and Zimbabweans, Iraqis and Afghans in the early 21st century.

▼ **Population Numbers of Different Ethnicities within Britain.**
Ethnic groups who migrated to Britain generations ago are now an established part of our population.

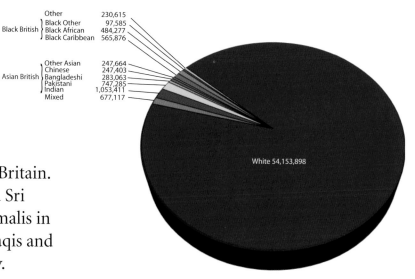

Other	230,615	
Black British { Black Other	97,585	
Black African	484,277	
Black Caribbean	565,876	
Other Asian	247,664	
Asian British { Chinese	247,403	
Bangladeshi	283,063	
Pakistani	747,285	
Indian	1,053,411	
Mixed	677,117	
White	54,153,898	

20

Where do immigrants settle?

When people arrive in Britain, they usually head to cities to find work, and settle near existing communities from their own cultures. London in particular is host to a high proportion of foreign immigrants. Approximately one third of the city's population is from an ethnic minority.

Emigration

Emigration is the outward flow of Britons who move to settle in other countries. In the past, people most commonly headed to old Commonwealth countries such as Australia, or New Zealand. However, now that EU borders have become more relaxed, more are heading to Europe, with France and Spain the second and third most popular choices after Australia.

CASE STUDY
Dispersal programme

The British government's 'Dispersal' programme was introduced in April 2000 to resettle asylum seekers in towns and cities across Britain, and to ease the burden on the areas currently hosting the majority of asylum seekers (in particular the southeast). There have been concerns about a lack of social integration and insufficient facilities for settlers, but in some areas suffering from a declining population the scheme has proved a success.

Up for discussion

The 'brain drain' is a term used to describe highly qualified workers, such as doctors and scientists, from less developed countries, coming to work in Britain and other more developed countries. What impact do you think this trend has?

▼ This busy London street shows the diversity of the city's population.

THE EUROPEAN UNION

May 2004 saw the addition of ten new countries to the European Union, and with it a wave of migrant workers looking for jobs in Britain. In 2007, Romania and Bulgaria also joined the union, which enabled their citizens to travel to Britain to find work.

Opening the borders

Britain's Worker Registration Scheme allows people from EU countries to work in the country. Britain was one of only three original EU countries, along with Ireland and Sweden, to open their borders to new workers; other member countries limited access to their job markets.

▼ Many British farmers have welcomed new workers from the EU because they couldn't find enough local people to do seasonal farming work.

Up for discussion

Do you think immigrant workers benefit the British economy? Should the government restrict the number of foreign workers entering the country, or should jobs go to the best-qualified people, wherever they come from?

► New cultures also bring with them new opportunities for business. This Polish delicatessen serves familiar foods to Poles working in Britain, and offers new tastes to locals.

Benefits

The British government estimates that in 2004, immigrant workers contributed approximately £500 million to the British economy. They say that new workers pay tax and national insurance and fill key jobs in areas where there are gaps. They claim that Britain benefits from the migrants' range of skills, from the expertise of skilled professionals, such as doctors and nurses, to low-skilled workers doing jobs that many British people do not want.

What do the critics say?

Between 2004 and 2006, 427,000 EU migrants registered to work in Britain. Some 36,000 dependents arrived with them, and 27,000 child benefit applications were approved. Many argue that this influx puts a strain on welfare services such as housing, education and healthcare. Many also believe that immigrants take jobs that would otherwise have been filled by British people.

JUST THE FACTS

- 82 per cent of migrants are aged 18–34.
- The ten countries who joined the EU in 2004 were: Poland, Estonia, the Czech Republic, Hungary, Latvia, Lithuania, Slovakia, Slovenia, Malta and Cyprus.
- Four in ten migrant workers are from Poland.
- 56 per cent of migrants find work in factories.

CASE STUDY
New EU states

Although the government believes the EU migrant worker scheme has been a success, many more people came to find work than they had expected. For this reason, when Romania and Bulgaria joined the EU in 2007, new laws restricted their access to the British job market for a period of seven years. Low-skilled workers are restricted to certain industries, while high-skilled migrants can enter only with specific visas.

CULTURAL IDENTITY

The number and diversity of British immigrants is ever increasing. With people from so many origins, what does it mean to be British?

British identity

One in 12 people in Britain was born overseas. Some people feel threatened by the arrival of so many new faces and believe that British identity is being lost. Others are excited by the opportunity of forming a new identity, encompassing new cultures and beliefs.

Valuable contributions

Ethnic minorities have contributed to all sectors of society, including business, the arts, sport, lifestyle and even cuisine. Curry, originating from India, is currently Britain's most popular food! The challenge for the government is to recognise these contributions, and the differences between cultures, at the same time as establishing a common identity.

Cultural integration

For those arriving on our shores, it is often difficult to find a balance between holding onto traditional cultures and values and finding a new sense of belonging. Effective

▶ Some non-Muslims argue that to integrate with mainstream Britain, this Muslim lady should be asked not to wear her veil.

multicultural policies and government support are essential in assisting groups to integrate with mainstream Britain.

Managing diversity

Cities such as London and Birmingham where immigration numbers are high have experience of managing ethnic diversity. But areas of Britain with fewer immigrants require help to understand the issues involved. This is becoming more important as new migrants head to smaller rural communities to work.

Discrimination

Some immigrants can feel discriminated against because of their colour, race or beliefs. Discrimination often occurs when people feel threatened; sometimes they

CASE STUDY
Extremism

Extremism can grow out of real or believed alienation from mainstream society. Children of immigrants can be particularly at risk from extremism, which can take many forms including political or religious extremism. At worst, some extremists can feel forced to take action against the society that they feel alienates them and disregards their values. High-profile examples of such extremist action include the 7 July London Underground bombings.

may not even realise they are being prejudiced. Anti-discrimination laws help outline what constitutes discrimination, for example hiring or not hiring someone based on what country they come from.

Up for discussion

- Can you think of some ways in which the government could help immigrants to integrate with British ways of life?

- Do you think ethnic minorities should be made to integrate into their adopted country?

▶ The annual Notting Hill Carnival in London started in the 1950s as a celebration of Caribbean culture.

AGEING POPULATION

By 2014, more people will be over the age of 60 than are under 16 years old in Britain. People are living longer and having fewer children. The 'baby boomer' generation is reaching retirement age. We are currently on the brink of an 'agequake'.

Baby boomers

High birth rates in the 1950s and 60s, followed by a drop in the 1970s caused a 'bulge' generation known as the baby boomers. Because of its vast size, this group has had a huge impact on society at every life stage. For example, at school age, more schools were needed to educate them. Once they passed through, schools were left empty. This population wave is due to enter retirement from 2010.

Living longer

Medical advances mean that people are dying more of conditions associated with old age than of diseases associated with middle age. The introduction of widespread immunisations for diseases such as diptheria and polio after World War Two led to a dramatic drop in deaths caused by infectious disease. Deaths are now most commonly caused by cancer, heart disease and circulatory conditions.

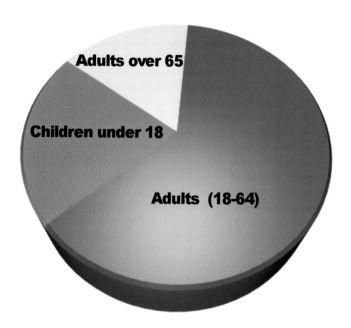

▲ The Dependency Ratio
The numbers of workers relative to the number of dependents (children and the elderly) is known as the 'dependency ratio'.

JUST THE FACTS

● One in four people over 85 live in care.

● The average age of retirement is 62.1.

● 25 per cent of deaths are attributed to cancer.

Cost of ageing

As the multitude of baby boomers starts to exit the workforce, we will be left with a declining working population relative to those needing support. Due to medical advances, people may now live far beyond the standard retirement age of 65. Pension payments for the recently retired and health and support services for the elderly in later stages of the life cycle are costs that will now need to be shouldered by a

IGNORE THIS POSTER.
IT'S GOT GREY HAIR.

Registered No. 261794

AGE DISCRIMINATION EXISTS. HELP US PUT A STOP TO IT.
www.ageconcern.org.uk/ageism

AGE Concern

smaller working group. Two key options have been identified to deal with this imminent problem:

- raising more taxes, or;
- raising the age of retirement, allowing more time to collect income tax and delaying the payment of pensions.

Older workers

Many people are keen to work beyond the retirement age. However, older workers may wish to work shorter hours than their younger colleagues, and they often juggle other commitments, such as caring for grandchildren, and therefore require flexible working options. The British government is doing its best to encourage employers to accommodate older workers. On 6 October 2006, it launched an anti-age discrimination policy, making it illegal for an employer to discriminate on the basis of age.

▲ The charity Age Concern has launched a high-profile campaign to combat age discrimination in the workplace.

Up for discussion

- **What are some of the implications of raising the retirement age?**

- **What skills can an older person bring to the workplace?**

27

LOOKING TO THE FUTURE

Statisticians predict that Britain's population will gradually increase to around 67 million inhabitants by 2031. What does this mean for the future of Britain?

A stable population...

Although Britain's population has experienced slight growth over the past ten years, our current population is relatively stable. Low birth rates, brought about by later marriage and women putting motherhood on hold until their careers are established, combined with increased life expectancy, means that the annual numbers of births and deaths are roughly equal. People's movements within Britain currently have the greatest impact on life opportunities and access to resources.

...Or a declining one?

However, while the social trend for smaller families means that birth rates are unlikely to increase, the death rate is due to rise soon as the baby boomer generation (see p.26) approaches the later life stages. Therefore it is possible that our population could decline in the future.

A smaller population may add to quality of life as competition for resources is reduced. However, the cost of an ageing population can outweigh the benefits, making it difficult for the working population to support elderly dependents.

Immigration contribution

Despite these projections, Britain's population has actually grown by 0.5 per cent a year since 2001. The main cause of the increase is immigration. The government is actively encouraging immigrants to come to Britain to boost the workforce and offset the cost of our ageing population. Immigrants often start a family, continuing this growth trend.

▶ **Population Growth in Britain, 1995–2005**
The British population is gradually increasing.

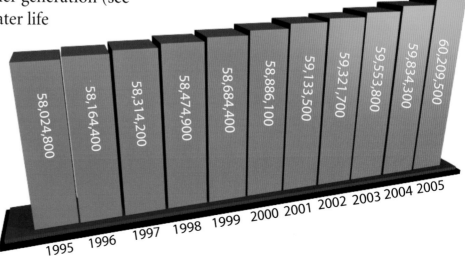

Year	Population
1995	58,024,800
1996	58,164,400
1997	58,314,200
1998	58,474,900
1999	58,684,400
2000	58,886,100
2001	59,133,500
2002	59,321,700
2003	59,553,800
2004	59,834,300
2005	60,209,500

Up for discussion

Some people predict a population explosion throughout the world, causing devastating environmental effects, and fierce competition for natural resources. How might Britain change if we had a sudden population spurt?

For the people

It is essential to try to predict how population might change so that we can plan for Britain's future. The right decisions will help to ensure Britain's ongoing prosperity and influential position on the world stage.

World stage

Although Britain's population, like those of most developed countries has remained relatively stable over the past decade, in less developed areas of the world the population has increased rapidly. Countries like China, India and Nigeria are growing extremely fast. This puts a great deal of pressure on the country's natural resources and increases competition for life opportunities such as jobs and housing. At the current rate, the United Nations expects that the world's population will swell from around an estimated 6.5 billion people in 2007, to 9.1 billion in 2050.

▶ A vision of the future? As urban space shrinks, and house prices rise, quick-thinking architects are converting shipping containers into affordable flats and office units.

GLOSSARY

Asylum seeker A person who is attempting to secure status as a political refugee.

Baby boomers The large group of people born during the period of high birth rates immediately after World War Two.

Brownfield site Urban land areas or buildings that have become derelict and are suitable for redevelopment or regeneration.

Census The process of collecting data about every member of a population.

Civil partnership A legally recognised union for same-sex couples.

Civil registration The government system that records the major life events of its population, such as births, marriages and deaths.

Commonwealth An association of 53 countries, including Australia, New Zealand and India, that were formally part of the British Empire.

Demographics Characteristics of a population, for example average age, sex, wealth or nationality.

Dependent A person who relies on another for financial support.

Dependency ratio The balance between the number of dependents in a population and the number of workers who must support them.

Emigration The movement of people away from their native country.

Economic Union (EU) A union of 27 European countries that share some common governing principles including policies on trade, agriculture and defence.

Greenbelt policy The policy developed by the British government in 1955 which restricts urban development in rural areas.

Immigration The arrival of new people from other countries.

Industrial revolution A major shift in the way people earned money and made goods, from manual labour to machine-based industry, that began in Britain in the 18th century.

Migration The change in population caused by the movement of people from one country, or area within a country, to another.

Natural change The difference between the number of births and deaths within a period of time. This, combined with immigration and emigration, gives a total population.

Political refugee A person who has migrated to a new country because of persecution or war in their home country.

Population A number of people living in a place.

Population density The number of people relative to the size of the area they live in. High population density means many people live in a small area, low population density means a small number live in a large area.

Recession A period of declining economic activity.

Rural Country areas with low population density.

Sanitation Facilities that promote hygiene and prevent disease, for example rubbish collection and sewage disposal.

Urban City areas with high population density. In Britain, all settlements with populations over 10,000 people are regarded as urban areas.

Welfare Financial and social support offered by the government to those unable to support themselves for reasons such as old age, poverty or disability.

FURTHER INFO

Books

Human Geography: Change in the UK in the Last 30 Years, David Redfern, (Hodder Murray, 2002)
Earth's Changing Landscape: Population Growth, Philip Steele (Franklin Watts, 2004)
Population Growth, Issues Craig Donnellan (Independence Educational Publishers 2001)
Roots of the Future, Ethnic Diversity in the Making of Britain, Mayerl Frow, Matthew Brown, Judith Lynne Hanna (Commission for Racial Equality, 1996)
Sustainable Human Development: A Young People's Introduction, Peace Child International (Evans Brothers, 2003)
Understanding Immigration Iris Teichmann, (Franklin Watts, 2005)

Websites

news.bbc.co.uk/1/hi/uk/4045261.stm
Use the interactive pie chart to see how the UK's population is changing.

www.nationalgeographic.com/earthpulse
Informative and interactive site that provides information about global population densities, the impact of urban sprawl and information on other geographical issues including climate, resources and humans and habitats.

www.unicef.org/voy
UNICEF's Voices of Youth website covers issues affecting populations worldwide, including poverty, water scarcity, sanitation and disease, etc. A good site for extending some of the issues raised in this book.

www.cpre.org.uk/home
Site of the Campaign to Protect Rural England, a lobby group who campaigns to maintain the Greenbelt policy.

www.ageconcern.org.uk
This site highlights issues for the aged, including new legislation on age discrimination. Also a lobby group for the aged.

www.urcs-online.co.uk
Case studies of Urban Regeneration Companies projects throughout Britain.

www.statistics.gov.uk
Website of Britain's official statistics. Contains census data.

www.geographyinthenews.rgs.org
The Royal Geographic Society's website. Includes a good section on international migration.

www-popexpo.ined.fr/eMain.html
Gives you the world population when in the year that you were born, plus lots of fun facts about population data.

www.prb.org
International site of the Population Reference Bureau. This site aims to give up-to-date information on a global scale on population, health and the environment.

Note to parents and teachers: Every effort has been made by the Publishers to ensure that these websites are suitable for children, that they are of the highest educational value, and that they contain no inappropriate or offensive material. However, because of the nature of the Internet, it is impossible to guarantee that the contents of these sites will not be altered. We strongly advise that Internet access is supervised by a responsible adult.

INDEX

These are the lists of contents for each title in *British Issues:*

Future Energy
The importance of energy • The state of energy today • Declining fossil fuels • Climate change • The nuclear debate • Wind power • Water power • Power from the Sun • Power from the Earth • Energy from waste • Innovations • Saving energy • Government and citizen action

Population Change
Britain's changing faces • Measuring change • People in the past • Population at work • Changing families • New lifestyles • Life moves • Trading places • Immigrants and emigrants • The European Union • Cultural identity • Ageing population • Looking to the future

Sporting Success
2012 • A rich history • Governing bodies •Funding • Facilities • Sport and society • The business of sport • Success stories • Sport and education • Fair play • Sport and the media • Sport and national pride • Looking towards 2012

Sustainable Cities
What does it mean to be a sustainable city? • Urban versus rural populations • Planning sustainable cities • Urban regeneration • Issues in the south-east • Stuck in the city • City movers • Sustainable energy • Water • Dealing with waste • Urban wildlife • Cities of opportunity • Vision of the future

Waste and Recycling
What is waste? • Throwaway society • What happens to waste? • Why waste matters • Managing waste • Reduce and reuse • Recycle! • How recycling happens • Composting • Energy from waste • Why don't we recycle more? • Changing the rules • A way to go

Water
Desert Britain? • The water industry • Water supply • Household water • Industry and agriculture • A growing gap • Climate change • The cost of water • Saving water • Drinking water • Water and the environment • Planning for the future • New technology